FIVE MINUTE
FACES

FIVE MINUTE
FACES

by SNAZAROO

RANDOM HOUSE  NEW YORK

Editor: Jacqui Bailey
Accessories: Deri Robins
Face Painting: Lauren Cornell,
Lyn Muscroft, Carol Richards,
Kirsten Stewart
Design: Pinpoint Design Co.
Photography: Roger Crump
Cover Design: Terry Woodley

First American edition, 1992

Library of Congress Cataloging-in-Publication Data
Five-minute faces : fantastic face-painting ideas / by Snazaroo. —
    1st American ed.
        p. cm.
    Summary: Presents step-by-step techniques for creating face-
painting designs for parties, outings, or fund-raising events.
    ISBN 0-679-82810-9 — ISBN 0-679-92810-3 (lib. bdg.)
    1. Face painting—Juvenile literature. [1. Face painting.]
I. Snazaroo (Firm)
TT911.F58 1992
745.5—dc20   91-26669

Manufactured in Spain
10 9 8 7 6 5 4 3 2

ONTENTS

INTRODUCTION

For hundreds of years, people have painted their faces—to frighten their enemies, appease their gods, amuse their audiences, and just for fun. Today, experienced face painters are in huge demand at all kinds of events, ranging from children's parties and charity functions to street fairs and carnivals.

Modern face-painting materials make it possible for anyone to produce good, quick results. The water-based makeup that is now available is particularly effective and easy to use. Even if you are not especially artistic, you will have great fun copying the designs in *Five-Minute Faces* and, we hope, inventing new ones of your own.

Practice makes perfect

In this book we have tried to provide a variety of designs that are both popular and easy to do. Each face is clearly illustrated with a close-up photograph and accompanied by simple step-by-step instructions. With a bit of practice, each one really is possible to do in five minutes or less!

Most people are surprised to discover just how easily water-based makeup can be applied, and how quickly dramatic effects can be achieved. The simpler designs can be mastered in a matter of minutes, and as your confidence grows, you will find yourself painting more and more complex designs in less and less time.

Costume accessories

Finally, the right accessories will make an enormous difference to the finished result of your face painting. So alongside the painting instructions in this book you will find simple suggestions for creating a variety of hats and other accessories, ranging from a sparkly tiara to a furry lion's mane. We hope that making them will provide you and your family with some fun, as well as being a cheap alternative to the ready-made outfits that are available in stores.

It's a good idea to start a dress-up box, which you can fill with odd items of clothing from secondhand stores and thrift shops. Keep an eye open for old felt hats, feather boas, net curtains, clothes made from silky or shiny fabric, pieces of fur fabric, and trims of lace. Go to costume shops and discount stores for novelties such as party hats, false ears and noses, fake mustaches and glasses, glitter wigs, feathers, and masks.

Above all, we hope that you, your friends, and your family will find fun and inspiration in this book—as much as we have found in putting it together.

You will not need to buy vast amounts of expensive equipment, but the following items are more or less essential:

Water-based makeup

All of the faces in this book have been painted with water-based makeup. It can be bought as palettes or as individual pots of color. A basic palette of 12 colors should give you a reasonable start, although if you expect to do a lot of face painting, you will probably find the pots more economical. A few fluorescent colors are also available.

Water-based makeup can be applied quickly and easily. It dries fast and doesn't rub off. The colors can be mixed, just like ordinary water paints, and best of all, it just washes off with soap and water, even out of clothes—in short, it's very parent-friendly!

Until recently, water-based paints were available only from specialty shops selling theatrical products. To some extent this is still the case, although they are becoming more widely available.

It's best to keep your paints and other equipment together in a handy container. A fishing tackle box or small plastic toolbox is perfect for this.

Cream makeup and sticks

Basically we recommend you avoid these. The grease makeup sticks and crayons that are sold in many stores tend to be difficult to use and have a limited effectiveness. Fine lines are difficult to draw, and complicated designs are virtually impossible.

Cream theatrical makeup is oil based and is hard to remove. It gives a rather heavy effect and has a tendency to smudge and rub off. Also, the colors cannot be mixed, although they can sometimes be blended together on the skin.

Brushes and sponges

In order to make your face-painting technique as varied as possible, buy a selection of different-sized brushes.

It is best to buy high-quality artists' brushes or special makeup brushes. We recommend that you use oxhair or sable brushes, as these are both soft and firm and easy to use.

Sable brushes are much more expensive than oxhair, but they are more versatile—you will be able to draw thick and thin lines with the same brush. Your local art store will probably have brushes that are a mixture of sable and

nylon, and these are also very effective.

Special face-painting or makeup sponges are the best type of sponge to use, but if you find these hard to obtain, then try using a dish-washing sponge cut into wedges to give you a fine edge as well as a broad surface.

Glitter

Some of the designs in this book use glitter makeup. If you are going to use glitter to decorate your faces, invest in some proper glitter gel that is designed to be used on faces. Do not try gluing or sticking on the dry glitter, which is intended for decorating cards and paper, and can be bought in craft stores.

Make sure that the glitter gel does not go too close to the eyes. With very young children it is best avoided altogether. Glitter gel is available from stores selling theatrical products.

Extras

Ordinary makeup is not really practical for face painting, but it can be useful if you want an effect to be waterproof, such as for a photograph or in a play.

Putting streaks of color into your hair can add to the effectiveness of the face. The best way is to apply water-based makeup with an old toothbrush or a damp sponge. Colored hair sprays can look good, but they are difficult and messy to use and may stain your clothing. If you do use one, make sure it is nontoxic and washes out easily.

Finally, you will need a container of water to wash out your brushes and sponges, lots of towels and facial tissues, a mirror to see the final result, and plenty of towelettes—it's not easy to paint a dirty face!

Important

Before you start face painting, check for skin allergies or infections. Although professional water-based makeup is nontoxic and highly tested, never paint someone's face if any kind of skin problem is suspected. If in doubt, try a little on the inside of his or her wrist and leave it for a few hours to see if a rash develops.

Preparation

Make sure that all your brushes, sponges, and paints are clean, and lay them out on a fresh towel. The water must be changed regularly.

There is no need to put any cream or moisturizer on the skin before you begin. Water-based makeup is best applied directly onto clean, dry skin.

If you follow the basic guidelines given below, you will be well on your way to becoming a proficient face painter.

1. First, tie a towel around the person's shoulders to protect his or her clothing. Keep the hair away from the face with a headband or clips.

2. Keep the person steady by resting one hand on his or her head.

3. Always apply the base color first, using a damp sponge. Make sure that the sponge is not too wet, or the finished result will be very streaky.

4. To achieve a deeper color, allow the first coat to dry, and then apply a second coat.

5. On designs that have a variety of light and dark colors, always apply the lighter color first.

6. When applying color with a brush, keep strokes even and work in continuous lines. Avoid the temptation to sketch. Confidence will come with practice.

7. Keep your designs simple but effective. Always remember that the average small child will find it difficult to sit still for more than five minutes!

8. Small children are sometimes nervous about having their faces painted. Reassure them by talking continuously, and explain exactly what you are doing at each stage.

9. Take great care when painting around the eyes. When lining the top eyelids, ask the person to keep his or her eyes closed until the paint has dried. When you are painting along the bottom of the eye, ask the person to look up as you do so. Be careful not to put the paint too close to the eyes.

Note: Water-based makeup is also great for body painting! Use brushes to paint rings on fingers, wrist-watches and bracelets on arms, or a huge tattoo—the effects can be stunning.

To get you started, here is an example of how the tiger face on page 26 was painted, step-by-step.

1. First, a yellow base was applied over the whole face, using a damp sponge. To avoid a streaky effect, we made sure that the sponge was not too wet.

2. A barely damp sponge was used to blend orange paint around the outside of the face, over the cheeks, and up into the hair around the edge of the face. For a smooth effect, the strokes were worked from the inside to the outside of the face.

3. A size 6, or medium, oxhair brush was used to paint white eyes and the white cheeks. A neat result was achieved by first painting the white outline and then filling in with the same color.

4. The nose was painted black, using short, upward strokes. Black was also used to paint the mouth and whiskers and to outline the eyes. A red line was painted under the eyes while the model kept very still and looked upward. Finally, a fine brush was used to decorate the face with red, black, and white strokes.

There comes a point when the good face painter is ready to branch out beyond the family circle and offer his or her skills to the world at large. Even if you feel that your talents are too modest for you to make a living out of face painting, you may find that they are more than good enough for fund-raising purposes.

Putting your skills to work

Unless you live in an extremely remote area, you should be able to find hordes of willing customers. Get in touch with as many schools as possible—most areas have some kind of school fair or carnival happening at some time during the year. Church fairs and local charity functions are good events, too. Keep your eye on the local newspaper for forthcoming events.

You could consider promoting your services with a simple leaflet—make it as attractive as possible and circulate photocopies to all likely places.

If you are lucky enough to live in a holiday resort area, contact the holiday centers, amusement parks, and hotels. You may be able to arrange a regular face-painting slot in their weekly events program.

When the summer is over, there are ample face-painting opportunities at Halloween, Christmas fairs, toy stores, and children's parties. In fact, the face painter can keep going all year round!

Running a stall

At busy events it is important to stand out from the crowd. A costume is essential—a good eye-catcher could be a clown's outfit, complete with hat and brightly colored face. If you can persuade one or two helpers to hand out leaflets, make sandwich boards for them to wear as they circulate among the crowd. They should also, of course, be wearing colorful samples of your skills!

Sit the person on a high chair or stool to make him or her visible to passersby. Keep your face paints scrupulously clean and tidy. No one will want you to paint their child's face with dirty-looking materials!

Crowd control

Wherever you see a face painter you will see a line of children. Crowd control skills are essential here. For everyone's sake, try to keep the line orderly and make sure that no one pushes in.

If you can, have a row of seats and move each person up one at a time, or you could issue numbered cloakroom tickets and call out the number when you are ready. With a bit of luck and diplomacy, you should be able to keep even the smallest customer happy.

Workshops

Older children will enjoy trying their hand at face painting. You may like to consider setting up workshops through schools or community centers.

When you go along to the school or center to discuss the idea, take some photos of a few finished faces (these should be as simple and effective as possible). Also, write out a program for an hourly session beforehand.

CLOWN

1. Using a damp sponge, apply a white base.

2. Paint a pink outline above the eyes with a brush. Fill in the area with blue paint.

3. Paint a red nose, taking care not to paint underneath the nostrils.

4. Use a brush to outline the mouth in red, and fill in with the same color.

5. Decorate the cheeks with yellow circles and green tears.

The photograph below right shows an alternate design, using the same basic stages.

MAKE A CLOWN'S HAT

For a quick and easy clown's hat, you will need:
Old felt hat (try second-hand stores)
Colored felt
Glue
Pipe cleaner
Plastic flower
Thick yarn

1. Cut different shapes from the felt, and glue them to the hat.

2. Sew strands of the yarn under the brim of the hat for hair.

3. Attach the flower to one end of the pipe cleaner, and tuck the other end into the hatband.

MAKE A PIERROT HAT

You will need:
Thin white cardboard
Glue or tape
Black paper or felt
String

1. Cut the shape shown below out of cardboard.

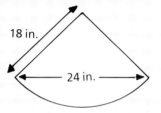

18 in.

24 in.

2. Glue or tape the edges together to make a cone.

3. Cut circles from black paper or felt, and stick to the hat, as shown.

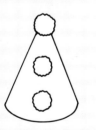

4. Make a small hole near the bottom of each side of the hat. Thread through enough string to fit comfortably under the chin, and knot in place.

1. Apply a white base with a damp sponge.

2. Blend in pink over the cheekbones, using a barely damp sponge.

3. Use a brush to paint silver shadows above the eyes.

4. Use a brush to paint high black eyebrows and black triangles under the eyes.

5. Paint a thin blue mouth, and add a blue teardrop on one cheek.

6. Finish by decorating with glitter gel, being very careful not to put the gel too close to the eyes.

1. Use a brush to draw the outline of the mask in pink, and fill in with the same color.

2. Paint blue crisscross lines with a thin brush.

3. Use a thin brush to paint white lace edging and feather.

4. Paint tassels at the sides of the mask.

5. Paint pink lips.

6. Decorate with glitter gel.

MAKE A SILVER HAT
You will need:
Thin cardboard
Silver paint
Glue or tape
Silver glitter

1. Cut cardboard to measure 26 x 6 in. Make cuts about 1 in. long and 1 in. apart along sides, as shown.

Cuts should be 1 in. apart and about 1 in. from the edge

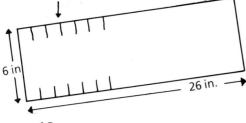

6 in

26 in.

2. Tape sides of the hat so it fits your head.

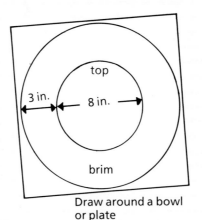

top

3 in.   8 in.

brim

Draw around a bowl or plate

3. Cut top and brim from one piece of card as shown. (Measurements here are approximate.)

4. Fold tabs on the hat.

5. Push the brim down over the hat. Glue or tape to the tabs. Glue or tape on the top of the hat.

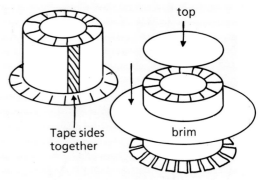

top

Tape sides together

brim

6. Paint the hat silver, and leave to dry. Coat with glue, and sprinkle with glitter.

1. Apply a white base with a damp sponge.

2. Using a barely damp sponge, blend in blue paint around the outside of the face.

3. Use a brush to paint silver above the eyes.

4. Use a brush to line the eyes in blue. Paint blue lips, eyebrows, and the design on the cheeks.

5. Apply a little red to the sides of the eyes and to the cheek design.

SNOW QUEEN MASK

Glitter wigs like the one in the picture are difficult to make and are best bought in discount stores. However, to add a touch of mystery, you could make this hand-held mask.

You will need:
Thin cardboard, about 4 × 6 in.
Silver paint
Glue or tape
Silver glitter
Scraps of lace or a paper doily
Thin stick, about 10 in. long

1. Draw a mask shape on the cardboard; cut it out. Cut holes for eyes.

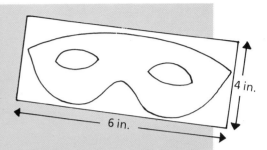

2. Paint the mask silver, and leave to dry. Cover with a thin layer of glue, and sprinkle evenly with glitter.

3. Glue scraps of lace or doily to edges of the mask. Tape or glue stick to one side, as shown.

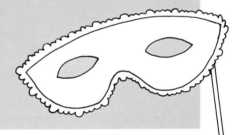

1. Apply a light brown base with a damp sponge.

2. Use a brush to outline the eyes in dark brown.

3. Paint blue and yellow zigzags on the forehead.

4. Use a brush and a variety of colors to decorate the rest of the face. Copy the design shown here, or use your own ideas.

# FLOWER GIRL

EASY AND QUICK!
1. Apply a thin yellow base with a damp sponge.

2. Using a brush, paint black lines above and below the eyes.

3. Paint the lips red.

4. Decorate cheeks with the designs shown in the picture.

FLOWER HEADDRESS

The Flower Girl in the picture wears silk flowers pinned to her hair. Instead, you could make the simple headdress shown below:

You will need:
Elastic headband
Colored tissue paper
Tape
Needle and thread

1. Cut the tissue paper into long strips, each about 14 x 2 in.

2. Roll each strip into a flower shape. Bind the base with tape.

3. Sew a cluster of flowers onto the headband.

To make different types of flowers, cut the edges of the strips in a variety of ways.

POLICE CLOWN

POLICECLOWN

1. Apply a white base with a damp sponge.

2. Use a brush to paint bushy green-and-blue eyebrows and blue triangles under the eyes.

3. Use a brush to paint a red nose and lips.

4. Finish by painting on black glasses and a curly beard.

JOKER

1. Draw a green line down the center of the face with a brush. Use a damp sponge to color one half green.

2. Use a damp sponge to color the other half of the face yellow.

3. On the green half of the face, brush gold over the lips and around the eye area.

4. On the yellow half of the face, paint a wiggly green eyebrow and green lips, as shown.

5. Outline the lips, golden eye, and green eyebrow in black, using a brush.

JOKER'S STICK

You will need:
Stick, about 16 in. long
2 brightly colored ribbons
Felt
The toe from a pair of tights
Cotton balls
Glue or tape
Needle and thread
5 bells

1. Bind ribbon around the stick until it is completely covered. Glue the ends in place.

2. Stuff the toe of the tights with cotton balls to make the head. Tie it to the stick with ribbon, leaving the ends loose.

3. Cut three identical triangles from the felt, and sew to the back of the stick's head. Sew a bell to the end of each triangle and to the ribbon ends.

4. Cut a mouth, nose, and eyes from the felt, and glue on to make the face.

1. Using a damp sponge, apply some red or purple next to one eye to make a bruise.

2. Dab black paint lightly over the chin with a sponge to look like stubble.

3. Use the brush to paint a bushy black eyebrow, an eye patch, a mustache, and a scar.

4. Paint the skull and crossbones in white; add the black details.

MAKE A PIRATE'S HAT
You will need:
Thin black cardboard, 28 × 18 in.
White paint
Stapler or tape

1. Fold the cardboard in half, and cut out two identical hat shapes.

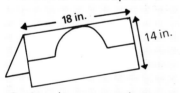

2. Staple or tape the two edges together, as shown.

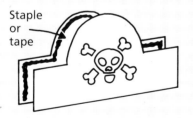

3. Paint a skull and crossbones in white paint on the front of the hat.

DRESSING UP AS A PIRATE

The following items make good pirate's gear:
Striped T-shirt
Old pants with tattered edges
Old vest
Long scarf tied as a sash around the waist
Gold clip-on hoop earring
Scarf to tie around the throat
Pirate's hat or a scarf to knot around the head
Chain necklaces
Cardboard sword

Landscapes are great fun to paint. They are not difficult and can be really effective. Practice this beach scene first before going on to create some of your own ideas. Remember to keep your designs as bold and simple as possible.

1. Use a damp sponge to color the blue sea and a slightly darker sky on the top half of the face. Use yellow to color sand on the bottom half. Wait until the background is thoroughly dry before adding the rest of the scene.

2. Paint the red sun and the reflection. Then add the black birds.

3. Finally, use a fine brush to add the two trees. Use different shades of green on the palm leaves and a dark color for the trunks.

LION

1. Apply a thin base of gold paint all over the face with a damp sponge.

2. Using a barely damp sponge, blend in yellow or brown around the outside of the face.

3. Using a brush, paint a black or dark brown nose, lips, and eyes.

4. Decorate the cheeks, chin, and forehead with short strokes of gold, brown, and yellow.

5. Hair can be combed into a wild mane, and streaked with gold paint using a sponge or an old toothbrush.

TIGER

1. Apply a yellow base over the whole face with a damp sponge.

2. Using a drier sponge, blend in orange around the outside of the face, over the cheeks, and into the hair.

3. Using a brush, paint white eyes and white around the mouth.

4. Paint short strokes of black around and underneath the eyes.

5. Paint black on the nose, using short upward strokes.

6. Paint black under the nose and over the lips.

7. Using a thin brush, paint the black whiskers.

8. Paint a red line under the eyes to give a fierce look. (Have tiger look up while this is done.)

9. Decorate with more fine brush strokes around the face, using red, black, and white paint.

MAKE A LION'S HOOD

You will need:
Beige fake fur about
40 × 20 in.
Thick cream-colored
yarn
Two ribbons
Needle and cotton

1. Fold the fur in half, and cut out two identical shapes, as shown.

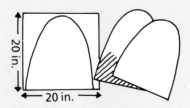

2. With the right sides facing, stitch the pieces together to make a hood.

3. Turn the hood the right side out. Slip it over your head, and lightly mark the face area with a pen.

4. Take off the hood. Cut a straight line up the front, from the bottom edge to the bottom of the face area. Cut out a hole for the face.

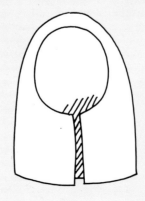

5. Sew the ribbons to the front edges, just below the face area, to fasten the hood under the chin.

6. Finally, sew on ears made from the same fabric, and add strands of the yarn to make the lion's mane.

For a tiger's hood, use tiger-patterned fake fur, and omit the mane.

GREEN CAT

1. Apply a pale green base with a damp sponge.

2. Using a barely damp sponge, blend in darker green around the outside of the face and down the nose.

3. Use a thin brush to outline the eyes in dark blue. Paint the tip of the nose, the mouth, and the spots above the mouth all the same color.

4. Decorate the face with small strokes of green and blue, as shown.

PINK CAT

1. Apply a white base with a damp sponge.

2. Using a barely damp sponge, blend in pale pink over the cheeks, forehead, and chin.

3. Using a brush, color the area above the eyes a slightly darker pink.

4. Outline the eyes in bright pink and purple, and paint feathery eyebrows.

5. Paint the lips bright pink.

6. Paint the tip of the nose black, and add a black line under the nose.

7. Use a thin brush to outline the lips in black. Paint black whiskers and black spots above the mouth.

8. Finish by decorating the forehead and cheeks, as shown. For an extra sparkle, add some glitter gel.

EASY AND QUICK!

1. Apply a yellow base with a damp sponge.

2. Use a brush to outline one eye in brown and to paint a large brown spot over the other eye. Add more spots.

3. Use a brush to paint a black nose and the mouth. Paint black feathery strokes underneath the mouth.

Use different colors and markings to invent your own breeds of dog.

EASY AND QUICK!

1. Apply a red base with a damp sponge.

2. Use a brush to outline the face in black and to draw a broad line down the middle of the face.

3. Use a brush to paint black spots.

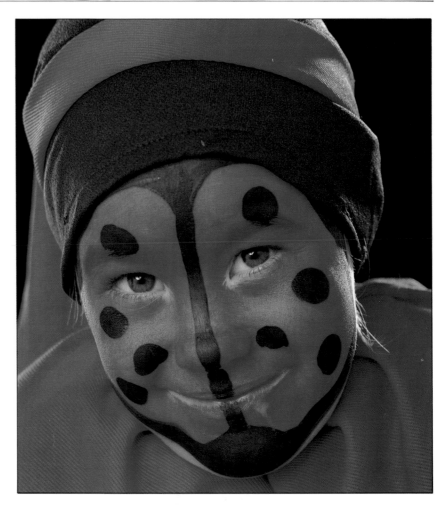

LADYBUG HEADDRESS

Stiff black cardboard
2 pipe cleaners
Black or red headband
Black felt
Tape
Glue

1. Cut two circles from the cardboard, each about 2 in. in diameter.

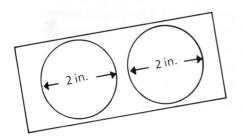

2. Fold felt in half. Trace around the cardboard circles and cut out, to make four felt circles.

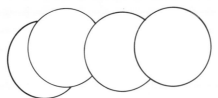

3. Glue a felt circle to each side of the cardboard circles.

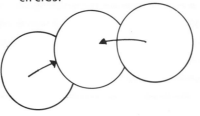

4. Tape a pipe cleaner to one side of each circle.

5. Tape the other ends of the pipe cleaners inside the headband.

6. For maximum effect, buy a red stretchy cotton ski hat from a sporting goods store. Put the antennae headband on top of the hat, and fold the edge over the band.

RABBIT'S EARS

For easy-to-make rabbit ears, you will need:

White fake fur
Pink fabric
Cotton balls
Plastic headband
Glue
Needle and thread

1. Glue a strip of fur over the headband, or sew a tube to slip over it.

2. Cut two ear shapes from the fur fabric and two matching shapes from the pink material, as shown.

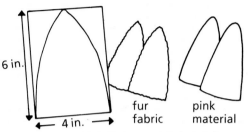

6 in.

4 in.

fur fabric

pink material

3. Sew each pink piece to a fur piece, with the right sides facing. Leave the bottoms of the ears open.

4. Turn the ears the right way around, and stuff lightly with cotton balls—you need just enough to make the ears stand upright.

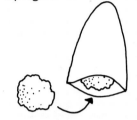

5. Sew the ears to the fabric on the headband, tucking in the bottom sides slightly.

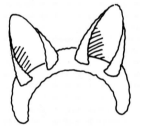

1. Apply a pink base with a damp sponge.

2. Using a barely damp sponge, blend in a small amount of red over the cheeks.

3. Using a brush, paint the white area around the eyes and the teeth.

4. Paint a small red heart on the tip of the nose with a fine brush.

5. Paint black eyebrows, eyelashes, and whiskers. Outline the teeth with a fine black line.

1. Apply a pink base with a damp sponge.

2. Using a thick brush, paint a black outline around the edge of the face, and fill in with the same color.

3. Use a brush to paint white eye shapes.

4. Use a thin brush to paint blue semicircles above the eyes. Lightly underline the eyes in the same color.

5. Paint red lips and a red heart shape on the nose.

6. Use a thin brush to outline the eyes, heart shape, and lips in black.

MAKE A PAIR OF MOUSE EARS

A mouse looks best in a long-sleeved T-shirt or leotard and a pair of tights or leggings of the same color. Attach a tail of yarn or string to the bottom of the tights or leggings.

To make ears, you will need:
Black construction paper
Headband
White paint
Tape or stapler

1. Cut out ears, as shown, and paint the center white.

2. Fold the bottom of the ear, and attach to headband with stapler or tape so ears stand up.

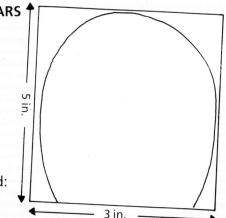

5 in.

3 in.

1. Apply a yellow base with a damp sponge.

2. Using a brush, paint black circles around the eyes, and fill in with the same color.

3. Use a brush to paint the black outline of the lower part of the bee's wings on the cheeks. Follow the lines of the cheekbones as a guide.

4. Use a thin brush to paint fine black veins.

5. Paint black lips and antennae above the eyes.

MAKE A PAIR OF BEE'S WINGS

A bee looks best in a striped yellow-and-black shirt worn over black leggings or tights. Or you could use fabric paints to paint black bands onto a yellow T-shirt, or sew yellow stripes onto a black T-shirt.

To make a pair of wings, you will need:
Black cardboard, about 28 × 8 in.
Wax paper
Glue
Needle and thread
Black felt-tip pen

1. Fold cardboard in half, and draw the wing shape shown below.

8 in.

14 in.

2. Cut out the outline of the wings, and open out. Cut away the center of each wing to leave a frame. Glue one side of the frame onto one side of the wax paper.

3. Trim away the excess wax paper. Turn the wings over, and draw veins on the wax paper with the black felt-tip pen.

4. Sew the middle of the wings to the back of the T-shirt.

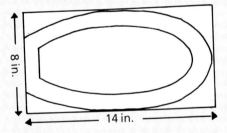

1. Apply a thin white base with a damp sponge.

2. Using a barely damp sponge, blend in turquoise around the forehead, cheeks, and chin.

3. Use a brush to paint the outline of the butterfly shape in blue, and fill in with the same color.

4. Blend in pink and yellow around the edges of the wings, as shown.

5. Paint pink lips.

6. Decorate the butterfly shape with glitter gel.

GOSSAMER WINGS

You will need:
Sheer fabric, about 24 × 16 in.
Colored felt-tip pens
Needle and thread

1. Fold the fabric in half, and draw the shape shown below.

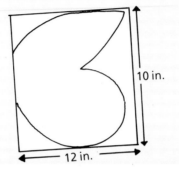

10 in.

12 in.

2. Cut out the wings, and open up.

3. Use felt-tips to decorate the wings.

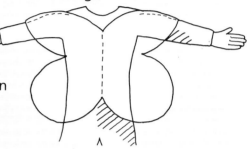

4. Sew the wings to the back and arms of the costume, as shown—a plain leotard or bathing suit worn over a T-shirt and tights is best.

There is no end to the designs that can be painted onto a face. Here you can see hearts, clouds, birds, rainbows, and sunshine. Other designs could feature flowers, balloons, kites, flags, fireworks, boats, and houses.

Pick up your own ideas by looking through picture books. Or try making up designs to suit a special occasion, such as Valentine's Day, 4th of July, or Earth Day.

1. Apply the base color, if any, using a damp sponge.

2. Use a brush or sponge to paint the main features of the design, such as the hearts or the rainbow shown here.

3. Use a thin brush to outline the eye area, if required.

4. Use a brush to color the lips.

You could try painting matching designs on other parts of the body, too, such as hands, arms, and ankles.

MAKE A RUFFLED CAP

You will need:
19 in. square of material
Elastic
Lace
Needle and thread

1. Round off the corners of the material to make a circle.

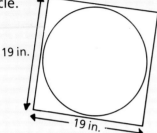

19 in.

19 in.

2. Sew the lace to the wrong side of the material, then press it flat on the right side.

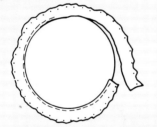

3. Find the right length for the elastic by measuring it around your head—don't make it too tight.

4. Pin it in place to the wrong side of the fabric before sewing. Sew the elastic in a circle, about 3 in. from the edge.

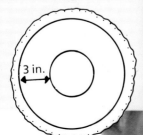

3 in.

VERY QUICK!

1. Using a brush, paint blue shadows above the eyes.

2. Paint rosy red cheeks and full red lips.

3. Use a fine brush to paint brown or black eyelashes above and below the eyes. Keep eyes closed until the paint has dried.

4. Finally, paint brown freckles over the nose.

1. Use a damp sponge to apply a thin white base.

2. Blend in pink over the cheeks.

3. Use a brush to paint pink around the eyes and up over the eyebrows, and paint pink lips.

4. Use a fine brush to paint thin black eyebrows and to underline each eye. Look up while you do this.

5. Paint a black beauty spot, and add some glitter gel above the eyes.

MAKE A TIARA

For a simple version of the tiara shown in the picture, you will need:
Strip of thin cardboard, about 24 × 3 in.
Tinfoil
Colored paper
Glue

1. Cut the tiara shape from cardboard, as shown.

3 in.
1½ in.
24 in.

2. Cover one side of the tiara with a thin layer of glue, and press down onto the wrong side of a sheet of tinfoil.

foil

3. Trim the edges.

4. Cut jewel shapes from the colored paper, and glue to the front of the tiara.

5. Glue or staple the two ends of the tiara together so that it fits your head.

QUICK AND EASY!

1. Apply a white base with a damp sponge.

2. Use a brush to paint the pink area above the eyes.

3. Paint red eyebrows and pink lips.

4. Underline the eyes in blue.

5. Use a fine brush and a mixture of bright colors to decorate the face with balloons and streamers, and the Happy Birthday message.

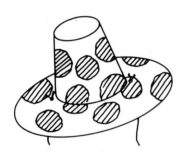

MAKE A PARTY HAT

You will need:
Empty yogurt container
White cardboard
Glue
Poster paints
Elastic

1. Draw around a saucer or bowl onto the cardboard to make a circle —it should be wide enough to make a brim of about 2 in. when the yogurt container is placed in the center.

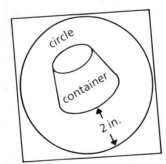

2. Cut out the circle, and glue the yogurt container to the center.

3. Paint the hat in bright colors, using thick poster paints.

4. Make a small hole on each side of the brim, and thread through enough elastic to fit comfortably under your chin. Fasten the elastic with a knot on each side.

1. Apply a white base with a damp sponge.

2. Use a brush to paint the area above one eye green and the other purple.

3. Paint the top lip purple and the bottom lip green.

4. Use a thin brush to underline the eyes in black.

5. Use bright or fluorescent colors to paint zigzags over the face.

6. Decorate with glitter gel, and add streaks of paint to the hair, using a sponge or an old toothbrush.

MAKE A PUNK OUTFIT

You will need:
Old clothes (preferably black)
Black plastic garbage bag
Belt
Safety pins

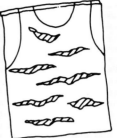

You could tear and pin the garbage bag too

1. Rip or cut holes in the clothes, and pin some of the holes together with safety pins.

2. Cut a vest shape from the garbage bag, with the closed end at the top. Don't worry about making the edges neat!

3. Wear the torn clothing, with the vest on top. Belt the vest around the middle.

4. For maximum effect, use face paints to draw a tattoo on one arm; paint fingernails with black nail polish; and use gel to shape hair into peaks.

KULL

1. Apply a white base with a damp sponge.

2. Use a brush to paint a black outline around the face.

3. Paint a black area around the eyes, the nose, and the mouth.

4. Paint a fine line from each corner of the mouth to the cheeks.

A SKELETON COSTUME

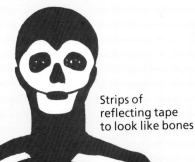

Strips of reflecting tape to look like bones

MONSTER

1. Use a damp sponge to apply a green base, spreading the color above the hairline.

2. Use a brush to paint red around the eyes and over the lips.

3. Outline the eyes and the red eye areas in black, and draw black feathery eyebrows. Outline the nostrils in black.

4. Paint white fangs, and add white dots within the red eye area.

5. Decorate the face with black lines and red dots.

You will need:
White or black cotton ski hat or bathing cap
Black tights or leggings
White briefs or bathing suit
Long-sleeved black T-shirt or leotard
Reflecting tape

1. Tuck all the hair into the hat or swimming cap.

2. Wear the black clothes, with the white briefs pulled over the top of the leggings or tights.

3. Stick strips of reflecting tape over clothes to indicate bones, as shown here. (For a more permanent costume, use white fabric paint.)

DRACULA

1. Apply a white base with a damp sponge.

2. Using a barely damp sponge, shade some gray into each side of the forehead, around the eye sockets, and into the hollows of the cheeks.

3. Paint the eyelids gray, using a brush.

4. Paint black eyebrows.

5. Use a fine brush to paint a thin red line under the eyes. (Have Dracula look up while this is done.)

6. Paint red lips. If you wish, paint red "blood" trickling from the corners of the mouth.

7. Paint white fangs.

DEVIL

1. Apply a red base over the face with a damp sponge.

2. Use a brush to paint around the eyes in gold.

3. Paint flames on the cheeks and forehead, using orange, yellow, and gold.

4. Paint a black pointed beard, fiendish eyebrows, and a black line at the outer corner of each eye.

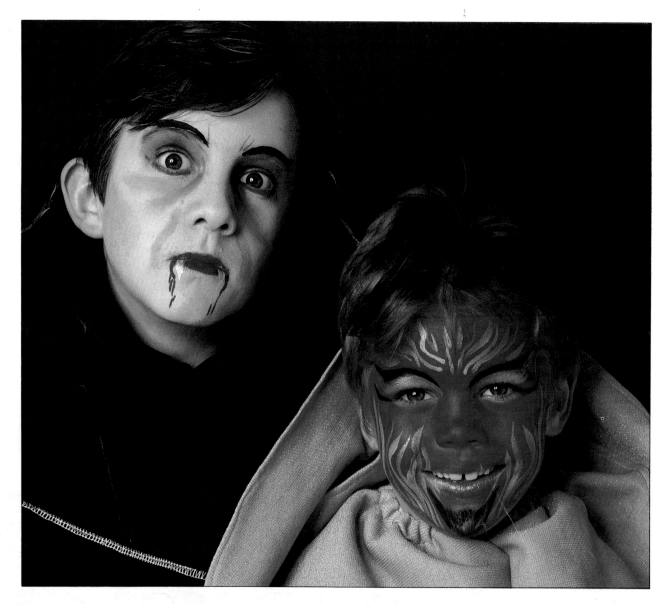

1. Apply a white base with a damp sponge.

2. Using a barely damp sponge, blend in blue paint around the edge of the face.

3. Use a brush to outline the black mask, and fill in with the same color.

4. Use a thin brush to paint the black cobweb and spider, and the lips.

5. Finish by adding a white flash to the mask at the outer corner of each eye, and paint white eyes on the spider.

A COBWEB COSTUME

You will need:
Gray or black sheer
  fabric
Ribbon
Fabric glue
Needle and thread
Glitter
Sequins
Tape measure

1. Measure the distance between your wrists when both arms are outstretched.

2. Mark the distance onto the sheer fabric, and cut out a circle to fit the same width.

3. Cut a hole in the center to fit your neck comfortably. Cut a slit down from the neck about 8 in. long, and sew a short length of ribbon to each cut edge.

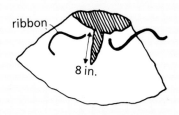

4. Lay the circle flat on the floor, and draw a web on it with the fabric glue. Sprinkle glitter over the glue before it has dried, and stick on some sequins. Leave to dry.

1. Use a damp sponge to apply a green base.

2. Use a brush to outline the eyes in black and to paint black eyebrows and lips.

3. Paint a black cat on the nose, a cauldron, and a spider.

4. Paint stars and the cat's bow tie and eyes white.

5. Paint the outer corners of the eyes and the flames under the cauldron red.

MAKE A WITCH'S HAT

You will need:
Thin black cardboard
Tape or stapler

1. Cut a cone shape from the cardboard. Tape edges together so it fits your head comfortably.

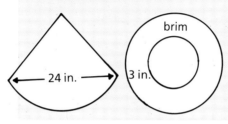

2. Trace the bottom of the hat and draw another circle 3 in. larger. Cut out

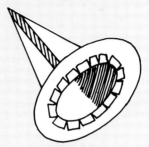

the brim, as shown.

3. Cut tabs 1 in. apart and 1 in. long around the bottom of the hat.

4. Slide brim over hat and attach tabs.

MAKE A CAPE

This useful cape can be made all green (for the Monster), with a red lining (for Dracula), all red (for the Devil), or black with a blue lining (for the Witch).

You will need:
Fabric, about a yard and a half
Silky lining material, about a yard and a half
Wide bias tape
Needle and thread
Cord or ribbon
Safety pin

1. Cut identical lengths from the fabric and the lining—measure the distance from the lower tip of your ear to your ankle for the length, and the distance around hips for the width. Add 1 in. all around for the hem.

2. Place the wrong sides of the fabric together. Hem the edges, turning the outer fabric in over the lining.

3. Sew the bias tape across the inside of the cloak, about 4 in. from the top. Use the safety pin to thread through the cord or ribbon.

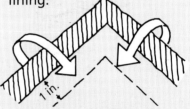